Maltese Dogs as Pets

Caring For Your Maltese

Maltese breeding, where to buy, types, care, temperament, cost, health, showing, grooming, diet, and much more included!

By Lolly Brown

Copyrights and Trademarks

All rights reserved. No part of this book may be reproduced or transformed in any form or by any means, graphic, electronic, or mechanical, including photocopying, recording, taping, or by any information storage retrieval system, without the written permission of the author.

This publication is Copyright ©2016 NRB Publishing, an imprint. Nevada. All products, graphics, publications, software and services mentioned and recommended in this publication are protected by trademarks. In such instance, all trademarks & copyright belong to the respective owners. For information consult www.NRBpublishing.com

Disclaimer and Legal Notice

This product is not legal, medical, or accounting advice and should not be interpreted in that manner. You need to do your own due-diligence to determine if the content of this product is right for you. While every attempt has been made to verify the information shared in this publication, neither the author, neither publisher, nor the affiliates assume any responsibility for errors, omissions or contrary interpretation of the subject matter herein. Any perceived slights to any specific person(s) or organization(s) are purely unintentional.

We have no control over the nature, content and availability of the web sites listed in this book. The inclusion of any web site links does not necessarily imply a recommendation or endorse the views expressed within them. We take no responsibility for, and will not be liable for, the websites being temporarily unavailable or being removed from the internet.

The accuracy and completeness of information provided herein and opinions stated herein are not guaranteed or warranted to produce any particular results, and the advice and strategies, contained herein may not be suitable for every individual. Neither the author nor the publisher shall be liable for any loss incurred as a consequence of the use and application, directly or indirectly, of any information presented in this work. This publication is designed to provide information in regard to the subject matter covered.

Neither the author nor the publisher assume any responsibility for any errors or omissions, nor do they represent or warrant that the ideas, information, actions, plans, suggestions contained in this book is in all cases accurate. It is the reader's responsibility to find advice before putting anything written in this book into practice. The information in this book is not intended to serve as legal, medical, or accounting advice.

Foreword

The Maltese is known for its silky white coat and bubbly personality, making it one of the most popular small-breed dogs out there. If you are thinking about getting a Maltese, you would be wise to learn everything you can about this smart and sassy breed and that is where this book comes in. In this book you will find a wealth of useful information about the Maltese breed including details tips for care. In reading this book you will learn everything you need to know to decide whether or not the Maltese is the right breed for you and, if it is, you will be well on your way to becoming the best dog owner you can be!

Table of Contents

Introduction 1
   Glossary of Dog Terms 3
Chapter One: Understanding Maltese Dogs 2
   Facts About Maltese Dogs 3
      Summary of Maltese Facts 5
   Maltese Breed History 7
Chapter Two: Things to Know Before Getting a Maltese 12
   Do You Need a License? 13
   How Many Maltese Dogs Should You Keep? 14
   Do Maltese Dogs Get Along with Other Pets? 15
   How Much Does it Cost to Keep a Maltese? 15
      Initial Costs 16
      Monthly Costs 19
   What are the Pros and Cons of Maltese Dogs? 22
Chapter Three: Purchasing Your Maltese 24
   Where Can You Buy Maltese Dogs? 25
   How to Choose a Reputable Maltese Breeder 29
   Tips for Selecting a Healthy Maltese Puppy 31
   Puppy-Proofing Your Home 34
Chapter Four: Caring for Your New Maltese 38
   Habitat and Exercise Requirements for Maltese Dogs 39

Setting Up Your Puppy's Area 41

Chapter Five: Meeting Your Maltese Dog's Nutritional Needs 44

    The Nutritional Needs of Dogs 45

    How to Select a High-Quality Dog Food Brand 46

    Tips for Feeding Your Maltese 49

    Dangerous Foods to Avoid 50

Chapter Six: Training Your Maltese 52

    Socializing Your New Maltese Puppy 53

    Positive Reinforcement for Obedience Training 55

    Crate Training - Housebreaking Your Puppy 56

Chapter Seven: Grooming Your Maltese 58

    Recommended Tools to Have on Hand 59

    Tips for Bathing and Grooming Maltese Dogs 59

    Other Grooming Tasks 61

Chapter Eight: Breeding Your Maltese 64

    Basic Dog Breeding Information 65

    Breeding Tips and Raising Puppies 66

Chapter Nine: Showing Your Maltese 70

    Maltese Breed Standard 71

    Preparing Your Maltese for Show 73

Chapter Ten: Keeping Your Dog Healthy 78

Common Health Problems Affecting Maltese Dogs 79
Preventing Illness with Vaccinations 89
Maltese Care Sheet 91
    1.) Basic Maltese Information 92
    2.) Habitat Requirements.. 93
    3.) Nutritional Needs 94
    4.) Breeding Information 95
Index 97
Photo Credits.. 107
References 111

Introduction

The Maltese is by far one of the most attractive and easily identified dog breeds out there. Known for its silky white coat and bubbly personality, the Maltese dog breed is great for singles and families alike. The Maltese is a member of the Toy Group but, despite its small size, these dogs have a large presence in the home, constantly seeking love and affection from their human counterparts.

What many people love about the Maltese breed is its friendly and playful personality. These dogs are full of life and their intense curiosity has been known to get them in trouble. Still, the Maltese breed makes a wonderful

Introduction

companion pet and they are a very popular breed for show. If you are thinking about getting a Maltese, you would be wise to learn everything you can about this smart and sassy breed – that is where this book comes in.

Within the pages of this book you will receive a wealth of knowledge and fun facts about the Maltese to give you a thorough understanding of the breed as a whole. Each and every Maltese has its own unique personality but the breed is known for certain physical and temperamental qualities. In reading this book you will learn everything you need to know to decide whether or not the Maltese is the right breed for you and, if it is, you will be well on your way to becoming the best Maltese owner you can be!

So, if you are ready to learn more about the Maltese breed simply turn the page and keep reading!

Introduction

Glossary of Dog Terms

AKC – American Kennel Club, the largest purebred dog registry in the United States

Almond Eye – Referring to an elongated eye shape rather than a rounded shape

Apple Head – A round-shaped skull

Balance – A show term referring to all of the parts of the dog, both moving and standing, which produce a harmonious image

Beard – Long, thick hair on the dog's underjaw

Best in Show – An award given to the only undefeated dog left standing at the end of judging

Bitch – A female dog

Bite – The position of the upper and lower teeth when the dog's jaws are closed; positions include level, undershot, scissors, or overshot

Blaze – A white stripe running down the center of the face between the eyes

Board – To house, feed, and care for a dog for a fee

Breed – A domestic race of dogs having a common gene pool and characterized appearance/function

Introduction

Breed Standard – A published document describing the look, movement, and behavior of the perfect specimen of a particular breed

Buff – An off-white to gold coloring

Clip – A method of trimming the coat in some breeds

Coat – The hair covering of a dog; some breeds have two coats, and outer coat and undercoat; also known as a double coat. Examples of breeds with double coats include German Shepherd, Siberian Husky, Akita, etc.

Condition – The health of the dog as shown by its skin, coat, behavior, and general appearance

Crate – A container used to house and transport dogs; also called a cage or kennel

Crossbreed (Hybrid) – A dog having a sire and dam of two different breeds; cannot be registered with the AKC

Dam (bitch) – The female parent of a dog;

Dock – To shorten the tail of a dog by surgically removing the end part of the tail.

Double Coat – Having an outer weather-resistant coat and a soft, waterproof coat for warmth; see above.

Drop Ear – An ear in which the tip of the ear folds over and hangs down; not prick or erect

Introduction

Entropion – A genetic disorder resulting in the upper or lower eyelid turning in

Fancier – A person who is especially interested in a particular breed or dog sport

Fawn – A red-yellow hue of brown

Feathering – A long fringe of hair on the ears, tail, legs, or body of a dog

Groom – To brush, trim, comb or otherwise make a dog's coat neat in appearance

Heel – To command a dog to stay close by its owner's side

Hip Dysplasia – A condition characterized by the abnormal formation of the hip joint

Inbreeding – The breeding of two closely related dogs of one breed

Kennel – A building or enclosure where dogs are kept

Litter – A group of puppies born at one time

Markings – A contrasting color or pattern on a dog's coat

Mask – Dark shading on the dog's foreface

Mate – To breed a dog and a bitch

Neuter – To castrate a male dog or spay a female dog

Introduction

Pads – The tough, shock-absorbent skin on the bottom of a dog's foot

Parti-Color – A coloration of a dog's coat consisting of two or more definite, well-broken colors; one of the colors must be white

Pedigree – The written record of a dog's genealogy going back three generations or more

Pied – A coloration on a dog consisting of patches of white and another color

Prick Ear – Ear that is carried erect, usually pointed at the tip of the ear

Puppy – A dog under 12 months of age

Purebred – A dog whose sire and dam belong to the same breed and who are of unmixed descent

Saddle – Colored markings in the shape of a saddle over the back; colors may vary

Shedding – The natural process whereby old hair falls off the dog's body as it is replaced by new hair growth.

Sire – The male parent of a dog

Smooth Coat – Short hair that is close-lying

Spay – The surgery to remove a female dog's ovaries, rendering her incapable of breeding

Introduction

Trim – To groom a dog's coat by plucking or clipping

Undercoat – The soft, short coat typically concealed by a longer outer coat

Wean – The process through which puppies transition from subsisting on their mother's milk to eating solid food

Whelping – The act of birthing a litter of puppies

Introduction

Chapter One: Understanding Maltese Dogs

Before you can decide whether or not the Maltese is the right breed for you, you need to learn everything you can about these dogs. Maltese dogs make wonderful pets, but they are not the right choice for everyone. In this chapter you will learn some basic facts about the Maltese breed to help you make your decision. You will also receive a history of the breed so you have a deeper context in which to view the breed as a whole. In the next chapter you will receive practical information about keeping Maltese dogs.

Chapter One: Understanding Maltese Dogs

Facts About Maltese Dogs

What many people love about the Maltese breed is its friendly and fun-loving personality. Many Maltese owners claim that their dogs retain their puppy-like attitude well into adulthood and that they make the best companions of any dog breed. It is true that the Maltese was bred to be a companion pet and it does have a very people-oriented personality. Maltese dogs are very prone to separation anxiety and they can become depressed and anxious when left alone for long periods of time.

Though the Maltese is a small-breed dog, it can have a big personality and it often develops a protective attachment to its owners. Maltese dogs generally stand 8 to 10 inches (20.3 to 25.4 cm) tall and weigh between 4 and 7 pounds (1.8 to 3.2 kg). These little dogs have an average lifespan of 12 to 15 years and many of them remain playful and eager to please throughout the entire lives. Maltese dogs are likely to follow their owners around the house, constantly seeking attention, and they are never happier than when they are napping on their human's lap.

Not only is the Maltese dog very lively and energetic, but it is a very smart breed as well. Maltese dogs respond very well to training and they love to perform special tricks. The earlier you start your Maltese with socialization and

Chapter One: Understanding Maltese Dogs

training, the faster he will learn. These dogs are very eager to please, so a little bit of attention and a treat is all they need to learn a new trick.

Maltese dogs are generally very friendly and affectionate with their families, though they do have a bit of a protective streak. These dogs have been known to bark at strangers and other dogs – some will even nip at strange dogs and people, even children, if they are not properly socialized. The Maltese makes a good watch dog because he will sound the alert if someone approaches the house, but he makes friends quickly once he learns that a visitor has the approval of his family. This breed can get along with other dogs and pets, though it is best if they are raised together and early socialization is still required.

In addition to its friendly personality, the Maltese is also known for its pure white coat of long, silky hair. These dogs are white all over with a single-layer coat (no undercoat) that is usually completely straight. The Maltese has small drop ears that are usually covered in long fur along with dark brown eyes and a black nose. The tail is well plumed and carried high over the back. Some Maltese dogs have a little bit of light tan or yellow coloration on the ears which is acceptable by AKC standards, but not preferred.

In terms of its exercise needs, the Maltese does very well with a daily walk. This breed may be energetic but it

Chapter One: Understanding Maltese Dogs

does not have excessively high needs for exercise. The Maltese is a healthy breed as well, having an average lifespan between 12 and 15 years. Some of the health problems to which this breed is prone are influenced by its small size – especially the size of its mouth and teeth. Other health problems known to affect this breed include glaucoma, hyperglycemia, portosystemic shunt, patellar luxation, progressive retinal atrophy, and shaker dog syndrome.

Summary of Maltese Facts

Pedigree: ancient breed, exact details are unknown

AKC Group: Toy Group

Breed Size: small

Height: 8 to 10 inches (20.3 to 25.4 cm)

Weight: 4 to 7 lbs. (1.8 to 3.2 kg)

Coat Length: long

Coat Texture: no undercoat; silky and smooth

Color: pure white; light tan or yellow on the ears is acceptable but not preferred

Eyes and Nose: brown eyes, black nose

Chapter One: Understanding Maltese Dogs

Ears: drop ears; small, low-set and well feathered

Tail: plumed, carried high over the back

Temperament: well-mannered, affectionate, lively, playful, energetic, loyal

Strangers: may bark at strangers; can be protective but makes friends quickly

Children: may not be a good choice for young children

Other Dogs: generally good with other dogs if properly trained and socialized; may bark at other dogs

Training: intelligent and very trainable

Exercise Needs: can be active and energetic but does not have high exercise needs; daily walk will be sufficient

Health Conditions: collapsed trachea, glaucoma, hyperglycemia, periodontal disease, portosystemic shunt, patellar luxation, progressive retinal atrophy, shaker dog syndrome

Lifespan: average 12 to 15 years

Chapter One: Understanding Maltese Dogs

Maltese Breed History

The Maltese is known among dog owners as an ancient breed, though it was not always called by the name it has now. The ancient Greeks called it the "Canis Melitaeus" while the Romans knew the breed as the "Roman Ladies' Dog". In English, the breed was nicknamed the "ancient dog of Malta" and the "Maltese Lion Dog". Though the breed has a very lengthy history, its current name is thought to have originated much more recently, given by The Kennel Club during the 19th century.

Because the Maltese is such an old breed, the exact details of its origins remain uncertain. It is commonly

Chapter One: Understanding Maltese Dogs

believed, however, that the breed descended from a Spitz-type breed that was developed by the Swiss Lake Dwellers for its small size. There is also evidence to suggest that the breed may have originated in Asia and that it might be related to the Tibetan Terrier. It is thought that the breed made its way into Europe through the Middle East, accompanying certain nomadic tribes in their migration across the continent.

The earliest record of the Maltese breed comes from a Greek amphora (a ceramic vessel used for the storage and transport of dry and liquid products) that was found in an Etruscan town called Vulci. The amphora depicted a Maltese-like breed labeled with the word "Melitaie". According to archaeologists, the amphora was made sometime around 500 BC. Other references to the Maltese breed have been found in ancient Greek and Roman literature as well.

The details of the Maltese's breed history remain fuzzy until the breed became established on the island of Malta. A beautiful island off the coast of Italy, Malta is where the breed truly began to flourish and it is the reason behind its modern name. Following its establishment in Malta, the Maltese breed moved throughout Europe and into Egypt where it became popular as a companion pet. There are numerous artistic depictions of the breed in the company of other small breeds like poodles and miniature spaniels.

Chapter One: Understanding Maltese Dogs

As the popularity of the breed increased, the breed was transported by traders throughout Europe and into Britain during the 1500s. It was during this time that the standard color for the breed – white – became established. The Queen of England declared the breed to be of royalty and it became a sign of status among English nobility to own one or more of these little dogs. Maltese dogs were treated royally, given lush sleeping quarters and human-quality food. Owning a Maltese became a status symbol during a time when only the wealthy could afford one.

The Maltese managed to survive the Dark Ages in Europe but it was nearly destroyed by selective breeding attempts to downsize the breed to the size of a squirrel. After the breed was nearly extinguished, breeders introduced poodles, miniature spaniels, and small dogs of Asian origin into the gene pool to restore the breed. These breeding practices resulted not only in the modern Maltese but the formation of several related breeds as well – the Bichon Frise, the Havanese, and the Bolognese.

The first Maltese appeared in the United States sometime during the late 1800s and they were first introduced at the Westminster Kennel Club show in the 1870s. By the late 1880s, the Maltese had won several all-breed shows and its popularity had become cemented in the United States. In 1888, the American Kennel Club accepted the Maltese and the rest is history. Today, the Maltese is

Chapter One: Understanding Maltese Dogs

consistently ranked among the top 30 breeds by AKC registration statistics.

Chapter One: Understanding Maltese Dogs

Chapter Two: Things to Know Before Getting a Maltese

Now that you know a little bit more about the Maltese breed and what makes it unique, you may have a better idea whether or not this is the right breed for you. Before you actually decide, however, you should consider some of the practical aspects of keeping this breed. In this chapter you will learn about licensing requirements for the Maltese as well as information regarding keeping it with other dogs and pets. You will also receive an overview of the costs associated with Maltese ownership and a list of pros and cons for the breed.

Chapter Two: Things to Know Before Getting a Maltese

Do You Need a License?

Before purchasing a Maltese dog, you should learn about local licensing requirements that may affect you. The licensing requirements for dog owners vary from one country to another so you may need to do a little bit of research on your own to determine whether you need a dog license or not. In the United States, there are no federal requirements for dog licensing – it is determined at the state level. While some states do not, most states require dog owners to license their dogs on an annual basis.

When you apply for a dog license you will have to submit proof that your dog has been given a rabies vaccine. Dog licenses in the United States cost about $25 (£16.25) per year and they can be renewed annually when you renew your dog's rabies vaccine. Even if your state doesn't require you to license your dog it is still a good idea because it will help someone to identify him if he gets lost so they can return him to you.

In the United Kingdom, licensing requirements for dog owners are a little bit different. The U.K. requires that all dog owners license their dogs and the license can be renewed every twelve months. The cost to license your dog in the U.K. is similar to the U.S. but you do not have to have your dog vaccinated against rabies. In fact, rabies does not

Chapter Two: Things to Know Before Getting a Maltese

exist in the U.K. because it was eradicated through careful control measures. If you travel with your dog to or from the U.K., you will have to obtain a special animal moving license and your dog may have to undergo a period of quarantine to make sure he doesn't carry disease into the country.

How Many Maltese Dogs Should You Keep?

The Maltese breed is very people-oriented and it requires a lot of personal attention. If you are worried that you might have to leave your Maltese alone for longer than a few hours on a fairly regular basis, it might be a good idea to get a second dog. Unfortunately, some Maltese dogs can be a little bit protective and nippy toward other dogs. Getting both of your Maltese dogs at the same time – especially as puppies – will help to prevent this from becoming an issue. Early socialization and training is important as well.

Another important factor to consider when thinking about Maltese dogs is whether you have young children in your family. Maltese dogs generally get along with older children who know how to properly handle a dog but they are prone to injury and rough treatment by young children. The Maltese may not understand that your children aren't trying to hurt him and he may nip at them out of self-defense which could scare or injure your kids.

Chapter Two: Things to Know Before Getting a Maltese

Do Maltese Dogs Get Along with Other Pets?

The Maltese breed may be small but these little dogs have big personalities. A Maltese will not hesitate to sound the alarm if a stranger approaches the property and they may even stand up to much larger dogs if they feel their family is being threatened. When it comes to getting along with other pets, each Maltese is different – their reaction will largely depend on socialization and training. Because Maltese dogs were developed as companion pets they do not have a strong prey drive so you probably don't have to worry about your Maltese chasing your cat or bothering other small animals. If you are worried about a Maltese getting along with other pets your best bet is to get a puppy and raise the pets together from an early age.

How Much Does it Cost to Keep a Maltese?

Before you commit to becoming a dog owner you need to make sure that you can provide for the needs of your dog. Not only does this include food and shelter, but you also need to provide training, grooming, and veterinary care. These costs can add up quickly so it is a good idea to learn what to expect in terms of both initial costs and monthly costs for Maltese ownership. In this chapter you will receive an overview of the initial costs and monthly

Chapter Two: Things to Know Before Getting a Maltese

costs to own a Maltese so you can determine whether it is practical for you.

Initial Costs

The initial costs for keeping a Maltese include those costs that you must cover before you can bring your dog home Some of the initial costs you will need to cover include your dog's crate, food/water bowls, toys and accessories, microchipping, initial vaccinations, spay/neuter surgery and supplies for grooming and nail clipping – it also includes the cost of the dog itself.

You will find an overview of each of these costs as well as an estimate for each cost below:

Purchase Price – The cost to purchase a Maltese will vary depending where you get it. If you decide to get a puppy, it is always best to purchase from a reputable breeder because it will reduce the risk for your dog developing an inherited disease. If you want an adult dog, you can adopt one from a local shelter for under $200 (£180) in most cases. The average cost for a Maltese puppy from an AKC-registered breeder is generally between $800 and $1,200 (£720 to £1,080), though show-quality dogs may cost more.

Chapter Two: Things to Know Before Getting a Maltese

Crate – Having a crate for your Maltese puppy is a must, especially if you plan to use the crate training method of housetraining. Your puppy's crate will become his personal space where he can relax and take a nap if he needs to. Because Maltese dogs remain fairly small you should only need to purchase one crate that will serve your puppy into adulthood. The average cost for a small crate is about $30 (£19.50).

Food/Water Bowls – To feed your Maltese you'll need a food and a water bowl. The cost for these items depends on the size and quality, but you should buy something made from either stainless steel or ceramic because these materials are easier to clean. Plan to spend about $20 (£18) on food and water bowls for your new puppy.

Toys – The Maltese is a very active breed so you'll need plenty of toys to keep him busy – having toys on hand will also help to keep him from chewing on your shoes or furniture. The cost for toys will vary depending on the type and number you buy, but budget a cost of about $50 (£32.50) to be safe.

Microchipping – In the United States and United Kingdom there are no federal or state requirements saying that you have to have your dog microchipped, but it is a very good

Chapter Two: Things to Know Before Getting a Maltese

idea. Your Maltese could slip out of his collar on a walk or lose his ID tag. If someone finds him without identification, they can take him to a shelter to have his microchip scanned. A microchip is something that is implanted under your dog's skin and it carries a number that is linked to your contact information. The procedure takes just a few minutes to perform and it only costs about $30 (£19.50) in most cases.

Initial Vaccinations – During your Maltese's first year of life, he will require a number of different vaccinations. If you purchase your puppy from a reputable breeder, he might already have had a few but you'll still need more over the next few months as well as booster shots each year. You should budget about $50 (£32.50) for initial vaccinations just to be prepared.

Spay/Neuter Surgery – If you don't plan to breed your Maltese you should have him or her neutered or spayed before 6 months of age. The cost for this surgery will vary depending where you go and on the sex of your Maltese. If you go to a traditional veterinary surgeon, the cost for spay/neuter surgery could be very high but you can save money by going to a veterinary clinic. The average cost for neuter surgery is $50 to $100 (£32.50 - £65) and spay surgery costs about $100 to $200 (£65 - £130).

Chapter Two: Things to Know Before Getting a Maltese

Supplies/Accessories – In addition to purchasing your Maltese's crate and food/water bowls, you should also purchase some basic grooming supplies as well as a leash and collar. The cost for these items will vary depending on the quality, but you should budget about $50 (£32.50) for these extra costs.

Initial Costs for Maltese Dogs		
Cost	**One Dog**	**Two Dogs**
Purchase Price	$800 to $1,200 (£720 to £1,080)	$1,600 to $2,400 (£1,440 - £2,160)
Crate	$30 (£19.50)	$60 (£39)
Food/Water Bowl	$20 (£18)	$40 (£36)
Toys	$50 (£32.50)	$100 (£65)
Microchipping	$30 (£19.50)	$60 (£39)
Vaccinations	$50 (£32.50)	$100 (£65)
Spay/Neuter	$50 to $200 (£32.50 - £130)	$100 to $400 (£65 - £260)
Accessories	$50 (£32.50)	$100 (£90)
Total	$1,080 to $1,630 (£972 – £1,467)	$2,160 to $3,260 (£1,944 – £2,934)

Monthly Costs

Chapter Two: Things to Know Before Getting a Maltese

The monthly costs for keeping a Maltese as a pet include those costs which recur on a monthly basis. The most important monthly cost for keeping a dog is, of course, food. In addition to food, however, you'll also need to think about things like grooming costs, annual license renewal, toy replacements, and veterinary exams. <u>You will find an overview of each of these costs as well as an estimate for each cost below</u>:

Food and Treats – Feeding your Maltese a healthy diet is very important for his health and wellness. A high-quality diet for dogs is not cheap, so you should be prepared to spend around $35 (£31.50) on a large bag of high-quality dog food which will last you at least a month. You should also include a monthly budget of about $10 (£6.50) for treats.

Grooming Costs – The Maltese has a very long, silky coat that will require professional grooming. Certain cuts and trims will make your dog's coat easier to maintain but a show-quality coat will need frequent brushing and grooming. You should plan a budget for the cost of professional grooming four times per year. The average cost for a professional grooming visit is between $50 and $75 (£32.50 – £68). This divided into 4 visits per year, equals a monthly grooming cost around $17 to $25 (£15 - £22.50).

Chapter Two: Things to Know Before Getting a Maltese

License Renewal – The cost to license your Maltese will generally be about $25 (£16.25) and you can renew the license for the same price each year. License renewal cost divided over 12 months is about $2 (£1.30) per month.

Veterinary Exams – In order to keep your Maltese healthy you should take him to the veterinarian about every six months after he passes puppyhood. You might have to take him more often for the first 12 months to make sure he gest his vaccines on time. The average cost for a vet visit is about $40 (£26) so, if you have two visits per year, it averages to about $7 (£4.55) per month.

Other Costs – In addition to the monthly costs for your Maltese's food, grooming, license renewal, and vet visits there are also some other cost you might have to pay occasionally. These costs might include things like replacements for worn-out toys, a larger collar as your puppy grows, cleaning products, and more. You should budget about $15 (£9.75) per month for extra costs.

Chapter Two: Things to Know Before Getting a Maltese

Monthly Costs for Corgi Dogs		
Cost	One Dog	Two Dogs
Food and Treats	$45 (£40.50)	$90 (£81)
Grooming Costs	$17 to $25 (£15 - £22.50)	$34 to $50 (£31 - £45)
License Renewal	$2 (£1.30)	$4 (£3.60)
Veterinary Exams	$7 (£4.55)	$14 (£12.60)
Other Costs	$15 (£9.75)	$30 (£19.50)
Total	$86 to $94 (£78 – £85)	$172 to $188 (£155 - £169)

What are the Pros and Cons of Maltese Dogs?

Before you bring home a Maltese dog, or any breed of dog, you should take the time to learn the pros and cons of the breed. Every dog breed is different so you need to think about the details to determine whether the Maltese is actually the right pet for you. You will find a list of pros and cons for the Maltese dog breed listed below:

Pros for the Maltese Breed

- The Maltese is a very small dog which makes it a great choice for urban or apartment life.

Chapter Two: Things to Know Before Getting a Maltese

- Maltese dogs are very loyal and affectionate with family – they make great companion pets.
- The Maltese is smart and eager to please which makes training fairly easy.
- Maltese dogs make good watch dogs because they bark at strangers when they enter their territory.
- The Maltese is very people-oriented so it will love spending time with you whenever possible.
- Maltese dogs are a very popular show breed so they are a good choice if you want to show dogs.
- The Maltese is one of the most popular dog breeds out there so finding one will be easy.

Cons for the Maltese Breed

- The Maltese has a very long, silky coat that will require daily brushing and frequent grooming.
- Maltese dogs require a lot of daily attention and may not do well when left alone for long periods.
- The Maltese can sometimes be nippy with other dogs if not properly trained and socialized.
- Maltese are generally not a good choice for families with young children – older children are okay.
- The Maltese does not have an undercoat so it may be sensitive to cold weather.

Chapter Three: Purchasing Your Maltese

Once you've decided that the Maltese is the right breed for you, the fun can really begin. Your first task is to figure out where you are going to get your Maltese – will you buy a puppy from a breeder or adopt from a local shelter? You also need to make sure that your home is "puppy-proofed" for the safety of your new puppy. In this chapter you will receive tips for choosing a Maltese breeder and for selecting a healthy puppy from a litter. You will also receive tips for preparing your home for your new puppy to ensure his safety.

Chapter Three: Purchasing Your Maltese

Where Can You Buy Maltese Dogs?

If you are sure that a Maltese dog is right for you, you need to start thinking about where you are going to get your new dog. Many people think that the best place to find a dog is at the pet store but, unfortunately, they are greatly mistaken. While the puppies at the pet store might look cute and cuddly, there is no way to know whether they are actually healthy or well-bred. Many pet stores get their puppies from puppy mills and they sell the puppies to unsuspecting dog lovers. Puppy mill puppies are often already sick by the time they make it to the pet store, often traveling across state lines to get there.

A puppy mill is a type of breeding facility that focuses on breeding and profit more than the health and wellbeing of the dogs. Puppy mills usually keep their dogs in squalid conditions, forcing them to bear litter after litter of puppies with little to no rest in between. Many of the breeders used in puppy mills are poorly bred themselves or unhealthy to begin with which just ensures that the puppies will have the same problems. The only time you should bring home a puppy from a pet store is if the store has a partnership with a local shelter and that is where they get their dogs. If the pet store can't tell you which breeder the puppies came from, or if they don't offer you any paperwork

Chapter Three: Purchasing Your Maltese

or registration for the puppy, it is likely that the puppy came from a puppy mill.

Rather than purchasing a Maltese puppy from a pet store, your best bet is to find a reputable Maltese breeder – preferably and AKC-registered breeder in the United States or a Kennel Club-registered breeder in the U.K. If you visit the website for either of these organizations you can find a list of breeders for all of the club-recognized breeds. You can also look for breeders on the website for other breed clubs like the American Maltese Association or the UK Maltese Club. Even if these organizations don't provide a list of breeders you may be able to speak with members through an online forum to find information.

If you don't have your heart set on a Maltese puppy, consider adopting a rescue from a local shelter. There are many benefits associated with rescuing an adult dog. For one thing, adoption fees are generally under $200 (£180) which is much more affordable than the $800 to $1,200 (£720 to £1,080) fee to buy a puppy from a breeder. Plus, an adult dog will already be housetrained and may have some obedience training as well. As an added bonus, most shelters spay/neuter their dogs before adopting them out so you won't have to pay for the surgery yourself. Another benefit is that an adult dog has already surpassed the puppy stage so his personality is set – with a puppy you can never quite be sure how your puppy will turn out.

Chapter Three: Purchasing Your Maltese

If you are thinking about adopting a Maltese, consider one of these breed-specific rescues:

United States Rescues:

Metropolitan Maltese Rescue.

<https://www.malteserescue.com/>

American Maltese Association Rescue.

<https://www.americanmalteserescue.org/>

Northcentral Maltese Rescue, Inc.

<http://malteserescue.homestead.com/>

Southern Comfort Maltese Rescue.

<http://www.scmradoption.com/>

Maltese Rescue California.

<http://www.malteserescuecalifornia.org/index.html?m>

Chapter Three: Purchasing Your Maltese

United Kingdom Rescues:

Maltese Club Welfare & Rescue.

<http://www.thekennelclub.org.uk/services/public/findarescue/Default.aspx?breed=6159>

The Little Dog Rescue.

<http://www.littledogrescue.co.uk/>

The Yorkshire Terrier & Toy Breed Rescue.

<http://www.yorkieandtoybreedrescue.co.uk/>

UK Maltese Club.

<http://www.themalteseclub.co.uk/home.html>

Chapter Three: Purchasing Your Maltese

How to Choose a Reputable Maltese Breeder

Finding a Maltese breeder may be as simple as performing and Internet search. If you want to find a reputable breeder, however, you may have to dig a little deeper. When you are ready to start looking for a Maltese puppy, compile a list of breeders from whatever sources you can and then take the time to go through each option to determine whether the breeder is reputable and responsible or not. You do not want to run the risk of purchasing a puppy from a hobby breeder or from someone who doesn't follow responsible breeding practices. If you aren't careful about where you get your Maltese puppy you could end up with a puppy that is already sick.

Chapter Three: Purchasing Your Maltese

Once you have your list of breeders on hand you can go through them one-by-one to narrow down your options. <u>Go through the following steps to do so:</u>

- Visit the website for each breeder on your list (if they have one) and look for key information about the breeder's history and experience.
    - Check for club registrations and a license, if applicable.
    - If the website doesn't provide any information about the facilities or the breeder you are best just moving on.
- After ruling out some of the breeders, contact the remaining breeders on your list by phone
    - Ask the breeder questions about his experience with breeding dogs in general and about the Maltese breed in particular.
    - Ask for information about the breeding stock including registration numbers and health information.
    - Expect a reputable breeder to ask you questions about yourself as well – a responsible breeder wants to make sure that his puppies go to good homes.
- Schedule an appointment to visit the facilities for the remaining breeders on your list after you've weeded a few more of them out.

Chapter Three: Purchasing Your Maltese

- o Ask for a tour of the facilities, including the place where the breeding stock is kept as well as the facilities housing the puppies.
- o If things look unorganized or unclean, do not purchase from the breeder.
- o Make sure the breeding stock is in good condition and that the puppies are all healthy-looking and active.
- Narrow down your list to a final few options and then interact with the puppies to make your decision.
  - o Make sure the breeder provides some kind of health guarantee and ask about any vaccinations the puppies may have already received.
- Put down a deposit, if needed, to reserve a puppy if they aren't ready to come home yet.

Tips for Selecting a Healthy Maltese Puppy

After you have narrowed down your options for breeders you then need to pick out your puppy. If you are a first-time dog owner, do not let yourself become caught up in the excitement of a new puppy – take the time to make a careful selection. If you rush the process you could end up with a puppy that isn't healthy or one whose personality isn't compatible with your family. Follow the steps below to pick out your Maltese puppy:

Chapter Three: Purchasing Your Maltese

- Ask the breeder to give you a tour of the facilities, especially where the puppies are kept.
    - Make sure the facilities where the puppies are housed is clean and sanitary – if there is evidence of diarrhea, do not purchase one of the puppies because they may already be sick.
- Take a few minutes to observe the litter as a whole, watching how the puppies interact with each other.
    - The puppies should be active and playful, interacting with each other in a healthy way.
    - Avoid puppies that appear to be lethargic and those that have difficulty moving – they could be sick.
- Approach the litter and watch how the puppies react to you when you do.
    - If the puppies appear frightened they may not be properly socialized and you do not want a puppy like that.
    - The puppies may be somewhat cautious, but they should be curious and interested in you.
- Let the puppies approach you and give them time to sniff and explore you before you interact with them.
    - Pet the puppies and encourage them to play with a toy, taking the opportunity to observe their personalities.

Chapter Three: Purchasing Your Maltese

- - Single out any of the puppies that you think might be a good fit and spend a little time with them.
- Pick up the puppy and hold him to see how he responds to human contact.
  - The puppy might squirm a little but it shouldn't be frightened of you and it should enjoy being pet.
- Examine the puppy's body for signs of illness and injury
  - The puppy should have clear, bright eyes with no discharge. The coat should be even and bright white, no patches of hair loss or discoloration.
  - The ears should be clean and clear with no discharge or inflammation.
  - The puppy's stomach may be round but it shouldn't be distended or swollen.
  - The puppy should be able to walk and run normally without any mobility problems.
- Narrow down your options and choose the puppy that you think is the best fit.

Once you've chosen your puppy, ask the breeder about the next steps. Do not take the puppy home if it isn't at least 8 weeks old and unless it has been fully weaned and eating solid food.

Puppy-Proofing Your Home

After you've picked out your puppy you may still have to wait a few weeks until you can bring him home. During this time you should take steps to prepare your home, making it a safe place for your puppy. The process of making your home safe for your puppy is called "puppy proofing" and it involves removing or storing away anything and everything that could harm your puppy. It might help for you to crawl around the house on your hands and knees, viewing things from your puppy's perspective in order to identify potential threats.

Chapter Three: Purchasing Your Maltese

<u>On the following page you will find a list of some of the things you should do when you are puppy-proofing your home:</u>

- Make sure your trash and recycling containers have a tight-fitting lid or store them in a cabinet.

- Put away all open food containers and keep them out of reach of your puppy.

- Store cleaning products and other hazardous chemicals in a locked cabinet or pantry where your puppy can't get them.

- Make sure electrical cords and blind pulls are wrapped up and placed out of your puppy's reach.

- Pick up any small objects or toys that could be a choking hazard if your puppy chews on them.

- Cover or drain any open bodies of water such as the toilet, and outdoor pond, etc.

- Store any medications and beauty products in the medicine cabinet out of your puppy's reach.

Chapter Three: Purchasing Your Maltese

- Check your home for any plants that might be toxic to dogs and remove them or put them out of reach.

- Block off fire places, windows, and doors so your puppy can't get into trouble.

- Close off any stairwells and block the entry to rooms where you do not want your puppy to be.

Chapter Three: Purchasing Your Maltese

Chapter Four: Caring for Your New Maltese

Once you bring your Maltese puppy home, the real work begins. To make sure things get off on the right foot you should make certain preparations to your home. For example, you need to set up a special area for your dog's crate as well as his toys and food bowls – you can use this area to contain your dog when you aren't home and it will become his special area where he can go if he needs some time to himself. In this chapter you will learn how to do this and you'll receive some basic tips for creating the ideal home environment for your Maltese.

Chapter Four: CARING FOR YOUR NEW MALTESE

Habitat and Exercise Requirements for Maltese Dogs

The Maltese is a small-breed dog so they do not require a lot of space. This is one of the reasons why Maltese dogs are popular for apartment and urban dwellers where space is limited. Even if your Maltese doesn't need a lot of space, he still needs enough exercise to work off excess energy. If you live in an urban area, you might not have a backyard where your Maltese can play. In cases like his, regular exercise is incredibly important – you'll need to take your dog on a daily walk for at least 30 minutes.

To make your Maltese comfortable and to ensure that he feels at-home, you will need to provide him with certain things. A crate is one of the most important things you will need when you bring your new Maltese puppy home. Not only will it be a place for your puppy to sleep, but it will also be a place where you can confine him during the times when you are away from home or when you cannot keep a close eye on him. Your puppy will also need some other basic things like a water bowl, a food bowl, a collar, a leash, toys, and grooming supplies.

When shopping for food and water bowls, safety and sanitation are the top two considerations. Stainless steel is the best material to go with because it is easy to clean and resistant to bacteria. Ceramic is another good option, though

Chapter Four: Caring for Your New Maltese

it may be a little heavier. Avoid plastic food and water bowls because they can become scratched and the scratches may harbor bacteria. For your dog's collar and leash, choose one that is appropriate to his size. This may mean that you will purchase several collars and leashes while your puppy is still growing. You might also consider a harness – this will be helpful during leash training because it will improve your control over your puppy and it will distribute pressure across his back instead of putting it all on his throat.

Provide your Maltese puppy with an assortment of different toys and let him figure out which ones he likes. Having a variety of toys around the house is very important because you'll need to use them to redirect your puppy's natural chewing behavior as he learns what he is and is not allowed to chew on. As for grooming supplies, you'll need a wire-pin brush for daily brushing as well as a slicker brush to work through tangles. You might also want a metal comb with wide teeth that you can use to work through stubborn mats and tangles.

Chapter Four: Caring for Your New Maltese

Setting Up Your Puppy's Area

Before you bring your Maltese puppy home, you should set up a particular area in your home for him to call his own. The ideal setup will include your puppy's crate, a comfy dog bed, his food and water bowls, and an assortment of toys. You can arrange all of these items in a small room that is easy to block off or you can use a puppy playpen to give your puppy some free space while still keeping him somewhat confined.

When you bring your puppy home you'll have to work with him a little bit to get him used to the crate. It is very important that you do this because you do not want your puppy to form a negative association with the crate.

Chapter Four: Caring for Your New Maltese

You want your puppy to learn that the crate is his own special place, a place where he can go to relax and take a nap if he wants to. If you use the crate as punishment, your puppy will not want to use it.

To get your puppy used to the crate, try tossing a few treats into it and let him go fish them out. Feeding your puppy his meals in the crate with the door open will be helpful as well. You can also incorporate the crate into your playtime, tossing toys into the crate or hiding treats under a blanket in the crate. As your puppy gets used to the crate you can start keeping him in it with the door closed for short periods of time, working your way up to longer periods. Just be sure to let your puppy outside before and after you confine him and never force him to stay in the crate for longer than he is physically capable of holding his bowels and his bladder.

Chapter Four: Caring for Your New Maltese

Chapter Five: Meeting Your Maltese Dog's Nutritional Needs

One of your most basic responsibilities as a dog owner is feeding your dog. Choosing a commercial dog food for your Maltese is not as simple as just walking into a pet store and picking out the first bag you see. Dog food varies greatly in terms of quality from one brand to another – even from one recipe to another. In this chapter you will learn about your dog's nutritional needs and receive tips for choosing a high-quality dog food. You will also receive general tips for feeding your Maltese.

Chapter Five Meeting Your Corgi's Nutritional Needs

The Nutritional Needs of Dogs

Like all mammals, dogs require a balance of protein, carbohydrate and fat in their diets – this is in addition to essential vitamins and minerals. It is important to understand, however, that your dog's nutritional needs are very different from your own. For dogs, protein is the most important nutritional consideration followed by fat and then carbohydrates. In order to keep your dog healthy you need to create a diet that provides the optimal levels of these three macronutrients.

The portion of your dog's diet that comes from protein should be made up of animal sources like meat, poultry, and fish as well as meat meals. Protein is made up of amino acids which are the building blocks that make up your Maltese's tissues and cells. It also provides some energy for your dog. The most highly concentrated type of energy your Maltese needs, however, is fat. This nutrient is particularly important for small-breed dogs because they have very fast metabolisms and therefore very high needs for energy.

Consider this – small-breed dogs have higher needs for calories by bodyweight than large dogs. A large-breed dog like a 110-pound Akita, for example, might need a total daily calorie intake of 2,500 calories, but that only amounts

Chapter Five Meeting Your Corgi's Nutritional Needs

to about 23 calories per pound of bodyweight. A 5 ½ pound Maltese, on the other hand, might only need 250 calories per day but that equates to about 45 calories per pound of its total bodyweight. A significant portion of these calories needs to come from fat in order to meet your dog's nutritional needs.

In addition to protein and fat, your Maltese also needs carbohydrates to provide dietary fiber and various vitamins and minerals. Dogs do not have a specific need for carbohydrates but they should always come from digestible sources since a dog's digestive tract is not designed to process plant foods as effectively as protein and fat. Your dog also needs plenty of fresh water on a daily basis as well as key vitamins and minerals.

How to Select a High-Quality Dog Food Brand

Chapter Five Meeting Your Corgi's Nutritional Needs

Shopping for dog food can be difficult for some dog owners simply because there are so many different options to choose from. If you walk into your local pet store you will see multiple aisles filled with bags of dog food from different brands and most brands offer a number of different formulas. So how do you choose a healthy dog food for your Maltese dog?

The best place to start when shopping for dog food is to read the dog food label. Pet food in the United States is loosely regulated by the American Association of Feed Control Officials (AAFCO) and they evaluate commercial dog food products according to their ability to meet the basic nutritional needs of dogs in various life stages. If the product meets these basic needs, the label will carry some kind of statement from AAFCO like this:

> "[Product Name] is formulated to meet the nutritional levels established by the AAFCO Dog Food nutrient profiles for [Life Stage]."

If the dog food product you are looking at contains this statement you can move on to reading the ingredients list. Dog food labels are organized in descending order by volume. This means that the ingredients at the top of the list are used in higher quantities than the ingredients at the end

Chapter Five Meeting Your Corgi's Nutritional Needs

of the list. This being the case, you want to see high-quality sources of animal protein at the beginning of the list. Things like fresh meat, poultry or fish are excellent ingredients but they contain about 80% water. After the product is cooked, the actual volume and protein content of the ingredient will be less. Meat meals (like chicken meal or salmon meal) have already been cooked down so they contain up to 300% more protein by weight than fresh meats.

In addition to high-quality animal proteins, you want to check the ingredients list for digestible carbohydrates and healthy fats. For dogs, digestible carbohydrates include things like brown rice and oatmeal, as long as they have been cooked properly. You can also look for gluten-free and grain-free options like sweet potato and tapioca. It is best to avoid products that are made with corn, wheat, or soy ingredients because they are low in nutritional value and may trigger food allergies in your dog.

In terms of fat, you want to see at least one animal source such as chicken fat or salmon oil. Plant-based fats like flaxseed and canola oil are not necessarily bad, but they are less biologically valuable for your dog. If they are accompanied by an animal source of fat, it is okay. Just make sure that the fats included in the recipe provide a blend of both omega-3 and omega-6 fatty acids. This will help to preserve the quality and condition of your Maltese dog's skin and coat.

Chapter Five Meeting Your Corgi's Nutritional Needs

In addition to checking the ingredients list for beneficial ingredients you should also know that there are certainly things you do NOT want to see listed. Avoid products made with low-quality fillers like corn gluten meal or rice bran – you should also avoid artificial colors, flavors, and preservatives. Some commonly used artificial preservatives are BHA and BHT. In most cases the label will tell you if natural preservatives are used.

Tips for Feeding Your Maltese

Once you've chosen a healthy diet for your Maltese dog you need to know how much and how often to feed him. Because different dog food products have different calorie content you should follow the feeding instructions on the label as a starting point. Most dog food labels provide feeding instructions by weight, so make sure you know how much your Maltese weighs. It is also important to remember that these are feeding suggestions – you might have to alter the ration for your dog. If your Maltese starts to gain weight, decrease his daily ration a little. If he loses weight, increase it a little bit.

In addition to knowing how much to feed your Maltese you also need to think about how often to feed him. Most dog owners recommend feeding your dog twice a day. Small-breed dogs like the Maltese have very fast

Chapter Five Meeting Your Corgi's Nutritional Needs

metabolisms, however, so you might want to divide his daily portion over three small meals. As your Maltese puppy is growing you can feed him freely, allowing him to eat as much as he wants. Once he reaches full size, though, you should start rationing his food.

Dangerous Foods to Avoid

It might be tempting to give in to your dog when he is begging at the table, but certain "people foods" can actually be toxic for your dog. As a general rule, you should never feed your dog anything unless you are 100% sure that it is safe. <u>Below you will find a list of foods that can be toxic to dogs and should therefore be avoided</u>:

- Alcohol
- Apple seeds
- Avocado
- Cherry pits
- Chocolate
- Coffee
- Garlic
- Grapes/raisins
- Hops
- Macadamia nuts
- Mold
- Mushrooms
- Mustard seeds
- Onions/leeks
- Peach pits
- Potato leaves/stems
- Rhubarb leaves
- Tea
- Tomato leaves/stems
- Walnuts
- Xylitol
- Yeast dough

Chapter Five Meeting Your Corgi's Nutritional Needs

If your Corgi eats any of these foods, contact the Pet Poison Control hotline right away at (888) 426 – 4435.

Chapter Six: Training Your Maltese

The Maltese is a very intelligent breed which makes it fairly easy to train – it also helps that the Maltese is very eager to please and people-oriented. Still, training is something that you have to commit yourself to and you need to be consistent in order to see results. In this chapter you will learn some tips for socializing your Maltese puppy from a young age as well as tips for using positive reinforcement for obedience training. You will also receive instructions for the crate training method of housebreaking your puppy.

Chapter Six: Training Your Maltese

Socializing Your New Maltese Puppy

The first three months of life is when your Maltese puppy will be the most impressionable. This is when you need to socialize him because the experiences he has as a puppy will shape the way he interacts with the world as an adult. If you don't properly socialize your Maltese puppy then he could grow up to be a mal-adjusted adult who fears new experiences. Fortunately, socialization is very simple – all you have to do is make sure that your puppy has plenty of new experiences.

<u>Below you will find a list of things you should expose your puppy to for properly socialization:</u>

- Introduce your puppy to friends in the comfort of your own home.

- Invite friends with dogs or puppies to come meet your Maltese (make sure everyone is vaccinated).

- Expose your puppy to people of different sizes, shapes, gender, and skin color.

- Introduce your puppy to children of different ages – just make sure they know how to handle the puppy

Chapter Six: Training Your Maltese

safely.

- Take your puppy with you in the car when you run errands.

- Walk your puppy in as many places as possible so he is exposed to different surfaces and surroundings.

- Expose your puppy to water from hoses, sprinklers, showers, pools, etc.

- Make sure your puppy experiences loud noises such as fireworks, cars backfiring, loud music, thunder, etc.

- Introduce your puppy to various appliances and tools such as blenders, lawn mowers, vacuums, etc.

- Walk your puppy with different types of harnesses, collars, and leashes.

- Once he is old enough, take your puppy to the dog park to interact with other dogs.

Chapter Six: Training Your Maltese

Positive Reinforcement for Obedience Training

Training a dog is not as difficult as many people think – it all has to do with the rewards. Think about this – if you want someone do so something for you, you probably offer them something in return. The same concept is true for dog training – if you reward your dog for performing a particular behavior then he will be more likely to repeat it in the future. This is called positive reinforcement training and it is one of the simplest yet most effective training methods you can use as a dog owner.

The key to success with dog training is two-fold. For one thing, you need to make sure that your dog understands what it is you are asking him. If he doesn't know what a command means it doesn't matter how many times you say it, he won't respond correctly. In order to teach your dog what a command means you should give it and then guide him to perform the behavior. Once he does, immediately give him a treat and praise him – the sooner you reward after identifying the desired behavior, the faster your puppy will learn.

The second key to success in dog training is consistency. While your puppy is learning basic obedience commands you need to use the same commands each and every time and you need to be consistent in rewarding him. If you maintain consistency it should only take a few repetitions for your puppy to learn what you expect of him. You can then move on to another command and alternate between them to reinforce your puppy's understanding. Just be sure to keep your training sessions short – about 15 minutes – so your puppy doesn't get bored.

Crate Training - Housebreaking Your Puppy

In addition to obedience training, house training is very important for puppies. After all, you don't want to spend your dog's entirely life following after him with a pooper scooper. The key to house training is to use your puppy's crate appropriately. When you are able to watch

Chapter Six: Training Your Maltese

your puppy, keep him in the same room with you at all times and take him outdoors once every hour or so to give him a chance to do his business. Always lead him to a particular section of the yard and give him a command like "Go pee" so he learns what is expected of him when you take him to this area.

When you can't watch your puppy and overnight you should confine him to his crate. The crate should be just large enough for your puppy to stand up, sit down, turn around and lie down in. Keeping it this size will ensure that he views the crate as his den and he will be reluctant to soil it. Just make sure that you don't keep your puppy in the crate for longer than he is physically capable of holding his bladder. Always take your puppy out before putting him in the crate and immediately after releasing him.

If you give your puppy ample opportunity to do his business outdoors and you keep him confined to the crate when you can't watch him, housetraining should only take a few weeks. Again, consistency is key here so always reward and praise your puppy for doing his business outside so he learns to do it that way. If your puppy does have an accident, do not punish him because he will not understand – he won't associate the punishment with the crime so he will just learn to fear you instead.

Chapter Seven: Grooming Your Maltese

Many people consider the Maltese a high-maintenance breed and they are right. The Maltese is a friendly and loyal companion, but his long, silky coat does require a lot of maintenance. Depending on the clip you choose for your Maltese, you may have to brush his coat daily and he might need monthly baths. If you intend to show your Maltese your grooming regimen will be different, involving more professional grooming and more frequent brushing. In this chapter you will learn the basics about grooming your Maltese.

Chapter Seven: Grooming Your Maltese

Recommended Tools to Have on Hand

If you plan to groom your Maltese yourself you will need certain tools and supplies. Even if you choose to have your dog professionally groomed, you should still have some supplies available for daily brushing and occasional bathing. <u>You will find a list of several recommended grooming tools and supplies below</u>:

- Wire-pin brush
- Metal wide-tooth comb
- Slicker brush (or undercoat rake)
- Small, sharp scissors
- Dog-friendly shampoo
- Nail clippers
- Dog-friendly ear cleaning solution
- Dog toothbrush
- Dog-friendly toothpaste

Tips for Bathing and Grooming Maltese Dogs

Because the Maltese has such a long coat, you may want to have it cleaned and trimmed by a professional groomer. Even if you do, you will still need to brush your dog's coat on a daily basis to prevent mats and tangles.

Chapter Seven: Grooming Your Maltese

Brushing your Maltese's coat is very easy – just start at the base of the neck and work your way along the dog's back, down his legs, and under his belly. Always brush in the direction of hair growth and move slowly so you don't hurt your dog if you come across a snag.

If you need to bathe your Maltese you will want to brush him first. When you are ready for the bath, fill the bathtub with a few inches of warm (not hot) water and place your dog inside. Use a cup to pour water over your dog's back or use a handheld sprayer to wet down his coat. Once your dog's coat is dampened, apply a small amount of dog-friendly shampoo and work it into a lather. After shampooing, rinse your dog's coat thoroughly to get rid of all the soap and then towel him dry. If it is warm you might be able to let his coat air-dry but if it is cold you should finish it off with a blow dryer on the low heat setting.

While you might be able to handle brushing and bathing your Maltese yourself, trimming his coat is probably best left to the professionals. There are several different clips that Maltese owners tend to prefer. If you plan to show your Maltese you should go with the standard cut which does not actually involve any trimming except for the fur on the feet to keep them neat.

A puppy cut is a popular choice for pet Maltese dogs because it is easy to maintain. This type of clip involves

Chapter Seven: Grooming Your Maltese

cutting the fur to an even length all over the body. The length of the cut is up to you but most Maltese owners that choose the puppy clip keep the coat about 1 inch long. The Teddy Bear cut is trimmed to ¼ inch on the back and side but the rest of the hair is left long. The face is trimmed into a round shape for this cut, making the dog look like a fluffy Teddy Bear. Another popular option is the Classic Bob in which the hair on the body is cut short but the fur on the head is parted into locks.

Other Grooming Tasks

In addition to brushing and bathing your Maltese, you also need to engage in some other grooming tasks including trimming your dog's nails, cleaning his ears, and brushing his teeth. <u>You will find an overview of each of these grooming tasks below</u>:

Trimming Your Maltese's Nails

Your dog's nails grow in the same way that your own nails grow so they need to be trimmed occasionally. Most down owners find that trimming their dog's nails once a week or twice a month is sufficient. Before you trim your Maltese's nails for the first time you should have your veterinarian or a professional groomer show you how to do it. A dog's nail contains a quick – the blood vessel that supplies blood to the nail – and if you cut the nail too short you could sever it. A severed quick will cause your dog pain and it will bleed profusely. The best way to avoid cutting your dog's nails too short is to just trim the sharp tip.

Cleaning Your Maltese's Ears

The Maltese has drop ears which means that they hang down on either side of the dog's head. This, combined with the fact that most Maltese dogs have a lot of hair on and in their ears, increases the dog's risk for ear infections. If the dog's ears get wet it creates an environment that is beneficial for infection-causing bacteria. Keeping your dog's ears clean and dry is the key to preventing infections. If you have to clean your dog's ears, use a dog ear cleaning solution and squeeze a few drops into the ear canal. Then, massage the base of your dog's ears to distribute the solution then wipe it away using a clean cotton ball.

Brushing Your Maltese's Teeth

Many dog owners neglect their dog's dental health which is a serious mistake. Small-breed dogs like the Maltese have a high risk for dental problems because their mouths are so

Chapter Seven: Grooming Your Maltese

small and their teeth can become overcrowded. You should brush your Maltese's teeth with a dog-friendly toothbrush and dog toothpaste to preserve his dental health. Feeing your dog dental treats and giving him hard rubber toys can also help to maintain his dental health.

Chapter Eight: Breeding Your Maltese

Breeding dogs is not something that should be taken lightly – it is a big responsibility to bring life into the world and it can be a risk for the female dog as well. If you aren't planning on breeding your Maltese, you should have him or her neutered or spayed before the age of 6 months. This will help to protect your dog against some serious diseases and it will also help to circumvent certain behaviors like urine marking. The information in this chapter will help you determine whether or not breeding is something you want to consider for your Maltese.

Chapter Eight: Breeding Your Maltese

Basic Dog Breeding Information

Before you decide whether or not to breed your Maltese, you should take the time to learn the basics about dog breeding in general. If you do not want to breed your Maltese, the ASPCA recommends having him neutered or her spayed before the age of 6 months. For female dogs, six months is around the time the dog experiences her first heat. Heat is just another name for the estrus cycle in dogs and it generally lasts for about 14 to 21 days. The frequency of heat may vary slightly from one dog to another but it generally occurs twice a year. When your female dog goes into heat, this is when she is capable of becoming pregnant.

When a female dog goes into heat there are a few common signs you can look for. The first sign of heat is swelling of the vulva – this may be accompanied by a bloody discharge. Over the course of the heat cycle the discharge lightens in color and becomes more watery. By the 10th day of the cycle the discharge is light pink – this is when she begins to ovulate and it is when she is most fertile. If you plan to breed your Maltese, this is when you want to introduce her to the male dog. If the isn't receptive to the male's advances, wait a day or two before trying again.

A dog is technically capable of conceiving at any point during the heat cycle because the male's sperm can

Chapter Eight: Breeding Your Maltese

survive in her reproductive tract for up to 5 days. If you don't plan to breed your Maltese you need to keep her locked away while she is in heat. A male dog can smell a female dog in heat from several miles away and an intact male dog will go to great lengths to breed. Never take a female dog in heat to the dog park and be very careful about taking her outside at all. Do not leave her unattended in your backyard because a stray dog could get in and breed with her.

If you want to breed your Maltese you will need to keep track of her estrus cycle so you know when to breed her. It generally takes a few years for a dog's cycle to become regular and some small-breed dogs go into heat more than twice per year. Keep track of your dog's cycle on a calendar so you know when to breed her. Tracking her cycle and making note of when you introduce her to the male dog will help you predict the due date for the puppies.

Breeding Tips and Raising Puppies

Chapter Eight: Breeding Your Maltese

After the male dog fertilizes the egg inside the female's body, the female will go through the gestation period during which the puppies start to develop inside her womb. The gestation period for Maltese dogs lasts for about 63 days but you won't be able to actually tell that your dog is pregnant until after the third week. By the 25th day of pregnancy it is safe for a vet to perform an ultrasound and by day 28 he should be able to feel the puppies by palpating the female's abdomen. At the six week mark an x-ray can be performed to check the size of the litter.

While the puppies are growing inside your Maltese's belly you need to take careful care of her. You don't need to feed your dog any extra until the fourth or fifth week of pregnancy when she really starts to gain weight. Make sure to provide your dog with a healthy diet and keep up with regular vet appointments to make sure the pregnancy is progressing well. Once you reach the fifth week of pregnancy you can increase your dog's daily rations in proportion to her weight gain.

After eight weeks of gestation you should start to get ready for your Maltese to give birth – in dogs, this is called whelping. You should provide your dog with a clean, safe, and quiet place to give birth such as a large box in a dimly lit room. Line the box with old towels or newspapers for easy cleanup after the birth and make sure your dog has access to

Chapter Eight: Breeding Your Maltese

the box at all times. As she nears her due date she will start spending more and more time in the box.

When your Maltese is ready to give birth her internal temperature will decrease slightly. If you want to predict when the puppies will be born you can start taking her internal temperature once a day during the last week of gestation. When the dog's body temperature drops from 100°F to 102°F (37.7°C to 38.8°C to about 98°F (36.6°C), labor is likely to begin very soon. At this point your dog will display obvious signs of discomfort such as pacing, panting, or changing positions. Just let her do her own thing but keep an eye on her in case of complications.

During the early stages of labor, your Maltese will experience contractions about 10 minutes apart. If she has contractions for more than 2 hours without giving birth, bring her to the vet immediately. Once your Maltese starts whelping, she will whelp one puppy about every thirty minutes. After every puppy is born, she will clean it with her tongue – this will also help stimulate the puppy to start breathing on its own. After all of the puppies have been born, the mother will expel the afterbirth and the puppies will begin nursing. The average litter size for the Maltese breed is 3 to 4 puppies.

It is essential that the puppies start nursing as soon as possible after whelping so that they get the colostrum. The

Chapter Eight: Breeding Your Maltese

colostrum is the first milk a mother produces and it is loaded with nutrients as well as antibodies that will protect the puppies while their own immune systems continue developing. The puppies will generally start nursing on their own or the mother will encourage them. After the puppies nurse for a little while you should make sure that your mother dog eats something as well.

When they are first born, Maltese puppies are very small – they may only weigh between 3 and 7 ounces (85 to 200g). Over the next week they will grow to 9 to 12 ounces (255 to 340g) and they will continue growing over the next several months until they zone in on their adult size. When Maltese puppies are born they will have some very fine hair but it isn't enough to keep them warm – your mother Maltese will help with that. The puppies will be born with their eyes and ears closed but they will start to open around the second or third week following birth.

Your Maltese puppies will be heavily dependent on their mother for the first few weeks of life until they start becoming more mobile. Around 5 to 6 weeks of age you should start offering your puppies small amounts of solid food soaked in broth or water to start the weaning process. Over the next few weeks the puppies will start to nurse less and eat more solid food. Around 8 weeks of age they should be completely weaned – this is when they are ready to be separated from their mother.

Chapter Nine: Showing Your Maltese

Showing your dog can be an exciting challenge for a dog owner and it is also a great way to improve your relationship with your dog. Maltese dogs are a beautiful breed which makes them very popular for show. Before you decide whether or not to show your own Maltese, however, you need to make sure that he meets the requirements set forth by the AKC for show. In this chapter you will learn the basics about the Maltese breed standard as well as some general tips to prepare for your first dog show.

Chapter Nine: Showing Your Maltese

Maltese Breed Standard

The AKC breed standard for the Maltese breed provides guidelines for both breeding and showing. AKC-registered breeders must select dogs that adhere to the standards of the breed and all Maltese owners who seek to show their dogs at AKC shows must compare them to the official breed standard as well. <u>Below you will find an overview of the standard for the Maltese breed</u>:

General Appearance and Temperament

The Maltese dog is gentle and affectionate – the perfect companion pet. This breed is covered from head to toe in long, silky white hair. The Maltese is gentle-mannered and trusting with a vigorous and playful side.

Head and Neck

The head of this breed is medium-long and proportionate to the size of the dog. The skull is slightly rounded and the muzzle of medium length and tapered. The ears are low-set and feathered, the eyes dark and round. The nose is black and the teeth meet in an edge-to-edge or scissors bite.

Chapter Nine: Showing Your Maltese

Body and Tail

The body is compact, the height equal to the length from the withers to the base of the tail. The back has a level topline with well-sprung ribs and a fairly deep chest. The tail is long-haired and plumed, carried high over the back.

Legs and Feet

The legs are fine-boned and feathered, the forelegs straight. The hind legs are strong and angled as the stifles and hocks, the feet small and round. The toe pads are black and the hairs on the feet may be trimmed neatly.

Coat and Color

This breed has a single coat over long, flat and silky hair that hangs almost to the ground. Hair on the head may be tied into a topknot or left hanging. Any degree of curliness or kinkiness is unacceptable and the color must be pure white. Light tan or lemon coloring on the ears is permissible.

Size

The weight must be under 7 pounds with a range of 4 to 6 pounds being preferable.

Chapter Nine: Showing Your Maltese

Gait

The breed moves with a smooth but jaunty gait. The forelegs are straight and free from the shoulders, the elbows held close. The hind legs move in a straight line. Cowhocks or hind leg toeing are considered faults.

Preparing Your Maltese for Show

Once you've determined that your Maltese is a good representation of the official AKC breed standard, then you can think about entering him in a dog show. Dog shows occur all year-round in many different locations so check the

Chapter Nine: Showing Your Maltese

AKC or Kennel Club website for shows in your area. Remember, the rules for each show will be different so make sure to do your research so that you and your Maltese are properly prepared for the show.

<u>Below you will find a list of some general and specific recommendations to follow during show prep:</u>

- Make sure that your Maltese is properly socialized to be in an environment with many other dogs and people.

- Ensure that your Maltese is completely housetrained and able to hold his bladder for at least several hours.

- Solidify your Maltese's grasp of basic obedience – he should listen and follow basic commands.

- Do some research to learn the requirements for specific shows before you choose one – make sure your dog meets all the requirements for registration.

- Make sure that your Maltese is caught up on his vaccinations (especially Bordetella since he will be around other dogs) and have your vet clear his overall

Chapter Nine: Showing Your Maltese

health for show.

- Have your dog groomed about a week before the show and then take the necessary steps to keep his coat clean and in good condition.

In addition to making sure that your Maltese meets the requirements for the show and is a good representation of the AKC breed standard, you should also pack a bag of supplies that you will need on the day of show. <u>Below you will find a list of helpful things to include in your dog show supply pack:</u>

- Registration information
- Dog crate or exercise pen
- Grooming table and grooming supplies
- Food and treats
- Food and water bowls
- Trash bags
- Medication (if needed)
- Change of clothes
- Food/water for self
- Paper towels or rags
- Toys for the dog

Chapter Nine: Showing Your Maltese

If you want to show your Maltese but you don't want to jump immediately into an AKC show, you may be able to find some local dog shows in your area. Local shows may be put on by a branch of a national Maltese breed club and they can be a great place to learn and to connect with other Maltese owners.

Chapter Nine: Showing Your Maltese

Chapter Ten: Keeping Your Maltese Healthy

Chapter Ten: Keeping Your Dog Healthy

When it comes to keeping your Maltese dog healthy there are a number of things you need to do. One of the most important requirements is, of course, feeding your dog a healthy and nutritious diet. In addition to proper feeding, however, you also need to provide your dog with regular veterinary care. Your veterinarian should see your dog once every six months to administer vaccinations and to check for health problems. In this chapter you will learn about some common health problems affecting the breed so you know what to look for. You will also receive a sample vaccination schedule like the one your vet will follow.

Chapter Ten: Keeping Your Maltese Healthy

Common Health Problems Affecting Maltese Dogs

The Maltese is an ancient breed which generally correlates with good overall health. However, the Maltese was subjected to inbreeding during the 1500s in attempts to breed it down to the size of a squirrel. Following its near-extinction, the breed was crossed with other small breeds which introduced some new blood into the gene pool. Today, the Maltese is generally a fairly healthy breed but all dogs are subject to developing certain health problems..

In this section you will receive an overview of some of the conditions most commonly affecting the Maltese breed. By educating yourself about the cause, presentation, and treatment for these common conditions you can help to keep your Maltese in good health for as long as possible. Some of the common conditions affecting Maltese dogs include:

- Collapsed Trachea
- Glaucoma
- Hypoglycemia
- Patellar Luxation
- Periodontal Disease
- Portosystemic Shunt
- Progressive Retinal Atrophy
- Shaker Dog Syndrome

Chapter Ten: Keeping Your Maltese Healthy

Collapsed Trachea

The trachea is the windpipe and it is a structure made up of rings of cartilage in the dog's throat. When those rings begin to collapse and the airway becomes obstructed it is called tracheal collapse – this is a common cause of airway obstruction in dogs like the Maltese. In most cases air flow is restricted but not completely blocked. As a result, the dog might make a honking noise as it breathes or it might start coughing. This condition is particularly common in small-breed dogs.

The exact cause for tracheal collapse in dogs is unknown but it is thought to be some kind of inherited abnormality. Dogs that experience tracheal collapse may have weaker tracheal rings which are prone to collapse following periods of excitement, intense exercise, or eating/drinking. In addition to the honking cough, Maltese dogs with tracheal collapse may also have decreased exercise tolerance, difficulty breathing, and blue or gray gums. A survey of these symptoms is generally how your vet will diagnose this condition. In terms of treatment, antibiotics, cough suppressants, and/or corticosteroids may be prescribed. Weight loss is also recommended for obese dogs. If the dog shows no improvement after a few weeks, surgical treatment may be the best option.

Chapter Ten: Keeping Your Maltese Healthy

Glaucoma

One of several eye problems to which the Maltese breed is prone is glaucoma. Glaucoma is a condition in which fluid fails to drain properly and it accumulates within the eye, causing an increase in intraocular pressure. Without treatment, this pressure will lead to permanent damage of the optic nerve which can then lead to blindness. This condition is common in certain breeds like the Maltese, Samoyed, and Siberian Husky and about 40% of dogs that develop glaucoma eventually go blind.

There are two types of glaucoma. Primary glaucoma is caused by the eye's inability to drain fluid and it might produce symptoms like excessive blinking, redness of vessels in the eye, cloudiness of the eye, and dilated pupil in addition to vision loss. Secondary glaucoma occurs as a result of an eye infection and common symptoms include redness of the vessels in the eye, increased eye pressure, constriction of the pupil, headaches, loss of appetite, and behavioral changes

Treatment for glaucoma generally involves medication to help reduce pressure in the eye. Other therapies may be required to correct the condition causing the fluid not to drain properly. In some cases, the eye must be removed. Most dogs adjust well to a loss of vision.

Chapter Ten: Keeping Your Maltese Healthy

Hypoglycemia

Also known as low blood sugar, hypoglycemia is a condition that is often linked to diabetes in dogs. When your dog eats, his body breaks the food down into glucose which it then uses for energy. If your dog's body has trouble absorbing the glucose, or if high insulin levels get in the way, it might lead to low blood sugar. Symptoms of low blood sugar in dogs include loss of appetite, changes in vision, disorientation, weakness, restlessness, heart palpitations, and occasionally seizures.

There are a number of potential causes for hypoglycemia and it is generally associated with a secondary condition like diabetes. There are two main treatment options for hypoglycemia. The first option is to give the dog some food or sugar to raise blood sugar levels immediately. The second option is to treat the underlying cause of the condition. Your veterinarian will be able to diagnose the cause of your Maltese's hypoglycemia and administer the proper treatment.

Chapter Ten: Keeping Your Maltese Healthy

Patellar Luxation

Patellar luxation is a musculoskeletal condition in which the patella (or kneecap) slides out of its normal anatomic position within the groove of the femur (thigh bone). This condition is one of the most common joint abnormalities in dogs and it is particularly common in small and toy breeds like the Maltese, Pomeranian, Yorkshire Terrier and the Boston Terrier. It is also more common in female dogs than in male dogs.

In the early stages of the condition, many dogs do not display serious symptoms. They might experience some soreness or tenderness after the patella pops back into place but they may still be able to walk normally. The more frequently the dislocation occurs, however, the more wear and tear on the bone and joint the dog will suffer. This leads to osteoarthritis and pain, potentially even lameness in the joint. The dog generally doesn't experience pain while the kneecap is dislocated, but he will when it pops back into its rightful place.

The cause of patellar luxation is usually the result of a genetic malformation or some kind of trauma. Unfortunately, medical treatments are rarely effective and surgery is usually required to achieve long-term relief. After surgery the dog will need to limit its mobility and regular vet check-ups are recommended.

Chapter Ten: Keeping Your Maltese Healthy

Periodontal Disease

Also known as gum disease, periodontal disease is incredibly common in dogs. In fact, most dogs develop some level of gum disease by the time they are three years old. In most cases, dogs with periodontal disease do not show any signs in the early stages. As the disease progresses, however, the dog might experience pain, eroded gums, and even tooth or bone loss. At this point, the only treatment option is to remove the affected teeth.

After your dog eats, saliva, food particles and bacteria accumulate on the surface of the teeth in a film called plaque. Over time, the plaque hardens into a calculus known as tartar which can then start to spread under the gum line and into the root of the tooth and the bone beneath. The bacteria can also make its way into your dog's blood stream, causing serious infections.

As periodontal disease progresses you may notice signs like bleeding or red gums, loose teeth, difficulty chewing, bad breath, or ropey saliva. It is very important that your dog gets regular dental checkups as part of his veterinary exams – you should also have your dog's teeth cleaned once a year. To maintain your dog's dental health, brush his teeth daily.

Chapter Ten: Keeping Your Maltese Healthy

Chapter Ten: Keeping Your Maltese Healthy

Portosystemic Shunt

Also known as PSS, a portosystemic shunt an abnormality in the portal vein. The portal vein is the vein that transports blood from the circulatory system to the liver for filtration. A portosystemic shunt occurs when an abnormality forms between the portal vein and another vein, causing blood to bypass the liver. Without proper filtration of the blood, the dog may develop symptoms like stunted growth, poor muscle development, behavioral changes, and seizures. In some cases, dogs don't develop symptoms until they are older.

In order to diagnose your dog with portosystemic shunt, your veterinarian will perform an exam and a medical history. He may also order tests like a complete blood count, urinalysis, and a bile acid test. With medication and dietary changes, most dogs with portosystemic shunt improve quickly. For those that don't, however, surgery may be required to repair the defect. In some cases, antibiotics are prescribed and lactulose might be needed to help reduce toxin absorption in the body. Most dogs that do require surgery for portosystemic shunt live long, healthy lives – the survival rate is over 95%.

Chapter Ten: Keeping Your Maltese Healthy

Progressive Retinal Atrophy

The Maltese is prone to several eye problems including progressive retinal atrophy, or PRA. This is a degenerative disease that affects the retina of the eye – the part of the eye that is sensitive to light. PRA generally occurs in both eyes at the same time and it may lead to total blindness, though it is not painful for the dog. In fact, many dogs adapt well to a loss of vision as long as furniture and objects are kept in the same location around the home.

There are several forms of PRA characterized by the age of onset and the rate of progression. In most dogs, the photoreceptors in the retina of the eye develop around 8 weeks of age. If the dog has PRA, the retinas might not develop as well or they could begin degenerating at this point. Dogs with PRA generally experience degeneration within two months of birth and most of them go completely blind within a year.

Though PRA is not painful for your dog, it does affect his ability to see. The outward appearance of the eye is generally normal (no tearing or inflammation) but you might notice signs of changing vision. For example, the dog might have trouble seeing at night or it might be reluctant to go down stairs. Eventually the pupil will become dilated and, in some cases, the lens becomes cloudy or opaque.

Chapter Ten: Keeping Your Maltese Healthy

Shaker Dog Syndrome

Also known as white shaker dog syndrome, shaker dog syndrome is a condition that causes full body tremors in certain small-breed dogs including the Maltese, Bichon Frise, Poodle, and West Highland White Terrier. This condition is caused by inflammation in part of the brain known as the cerebellum – this is the part that regulates coordination and voluntary muscle movement. Dogs of any color can develop this condition but it is most common in white dogs.

The cause for shaker dog syndrome is unknown but it is commonly associated with some kind of mild central nervous system disease or disorder. Body tremors are the most common symptom of this condition and it can be easy to mistakenly diagnose as anxiety or low body temperature. To diagnose this condition, your vet will perform a thorough exam and a medical history. He may also take a blood chemical profile and a blood count as well as an electrolyte panel and urinalysis.

Treatment for shaker dog syndrome usually focuses on dealing with the consequences of the tremors. Corticosteroids are commonly prescribed to reduce inflammation over a period of weeks. Most dogs start to recover within one week, though some never do. In some cases steroid treatment must be continued over the lifetime of the dog.**Error! Bookmark not defined.**

Chapter Ten: Keeping Your Maltese Healthy

Preventing Illness with Vaccinations

Providing your Maltese with a healthy diet and regular veterinary care are two of the most important ways to maintain his health – vaccinations are also important. Having your dog vaccinated will help to protect him from certain deadly diseases like rabies, distemper, and parvovirus. The vaccinations your Maltese needs may vary depending where you live since certain regions have a higher risk for certain diseases. Your vet will know which vaccinations your dog needs and when he needs them, but the vaccination schedule below will help you to keep track of when your Maltese needs to see the vet.

Chapter Ten: Keeping Your Maltese Healthy

To give you an idea what kind of vaccinations your puppy will need, consult the vaccination schedule below:

Vaccination Schedule for Dogs**			
Vaccine	**Doses**	**Age**	**Booster**
Rabies	1	12 weeks	annual
Distemper	3	6-16 weeks	3 years
Parvovirus	3	6-16 weeks	3 years
Adenovirus	3	6-16 weeks	3 years
Parainfluenza	3	6 weeks, 12-14 weeks	3 years
Bordetella	1	6 weeks	annual
Lyme Disease	2	9, 13-14 weeks	annual
Leptospirosis	2	12 and 16 weeks	annual
Canine Influenza	2	6-8, 8-12 weeks	annual

** Keep in mind that vaccine requirements may vary from one region to another. Only your vet will be able to tell you which vaccines are most important for the region where you live.

Maltese Care Sheet

In reading this book you have received a wealth of knowledge and useful information about the Maltese breed as a whole as well as details for its care. When you bring your own Maltese home you can continue to use this book as a reference. Rather than flipping through the entire book to find specific tidbits of information, however, you can use this chapter's care sheet to find the information you need at a glance. In this chapter you will find the most important details for basic care, habitat requirements, nutritional needs, and breeding information all in one place.

Maltese Care Sheet

1.) Basic Maltese Information

Pedigree: ancient breed, exact details are unknown

AKC Group: Toy Group

Breed Size: small

Height: 8 to 10 inches (20.3 to 25.4 cm)

Weight: 4 to 7 lbs. (1.8 to 3.2 kg)

Coat Length: long

Coat Texture: no undercoat; silky and smooth

Color: pure white; light tan or yellow on the ears is acceptable but not preferred

Eyes and Nose: brown eyes, black nose

Ears: drop ears; small, low-set and well feathered

Tail: plumed, carried high over the back

Temperament: well-mannered, affectionate, lively, playful, energetic, loyal

Strangers: may bark at strangers; can be protective but makes friends quickly

Children: may not be a good choice for young children

Other Dogs: generally good with other dogs if properly trained and socialized; may bark at other dogs

Training: intelligent and very trainable

Exercise Needs: can be active and energetic but does not have high exercise needs; daily walk will be sufficient

Health Conditions: collapsed trachea, glaucoma, hyperglycemia, periodontal disease, portosystemic shunt, patellar luxation, progressive retinal atrophy, shaker dog syndrome

Lifespan: average 12 to 15 years

2.) Habitat Requirements

Recommended Accessories: crate, dog bed, food/water dishes, toys, collar, leash, harness, grooming supplies

Collar and Harness: sized by weight

Grooming Supplies: wire pin brush, slicker brush, metal wide-tooth comb

Grooming Frequency: brush daily; professional grooming every 2 to 3 months

Energy Level: fairly low

Maltese Care Sheet

Exercise Requirements: 30 minute walk daily

Crate: highly recommended

Crate Size: just large enough for dog to lie down and turn around comfortably

Crate Extras: lined with blanket or plush pet bed

Food/Water: stainless steel or ceramic bowls, clean daily

Toys: start with an assortment, see what the dog likes; include some mentally stimulating toys

Exercise Ideas: play games to give your dog extra exercise during the day; train your dog for various dog sports

3.) *Nutritional Needs*

Nutritional Needs: water, protein, carbohydrate, fats, vitamins, minerals

Calorie Needs: varies by age, weight, and activity level

Amount to Feed (puppy): feed freely but consult recommendations on the package

Amount to Feed (adult): consult recommendations on the package; calculated by weight

Feeding Frequency: two to three meals daily

Maltese Care Sheet

Important Ingredients: fresh animal protein (chicken, beef, lamb, turkey, eggs), digestible carbohydrates (rice, oats, barley), animal fats

Important Minerals: calcium, phosphorus, potassium, magnesium, iron, copper and manganese

Important Vitamins: Vitamin A, Vitamin A, Vitamin B-12, Vitamin D, Vitamin C

Look For: AAFCO statement of nutritional adequacy; protein at top of ingredients list; no artificial flavors, dyes, preservatives

4.) Breeding Information

Age of First Heat: around 6 months (or earlier)

Heat (Estrus) Cycle: 14 to 21 days

Frequency: twice a year, every 6 to 7 months

Greatest Fertility: 11 to 15 days into the cycle

Gestation Period: average 63 days

Pregnancy Detection: possible after 21 days, best to wait 28 days before exam

Maltese Care Sheet

Feeding Pregnant Dogs: maintain normal diet until week 5 or 6 then slightly increase rations

Signs of Labor: body temperature drops below normal 100° to 102°F (37.7° to 38.8°C), may be as low as 98°F (36.6°C); dog begins nesting in a dark, quiet place

Contractions: period of 10 minutes in waves of 3 to 5 followed by a period of rest

Whelping: puppies are born in 1/2 hour increments following 10 to 30 minutes of forceful straining

Puppies: born with eyes and ears closed; eyes open at 3 weeks, teeth develop at 10 weeks

Litter Size: average 3 to 4 puppies

Size at Birth: between 3 and 7 ounces (85 to 200g)

Weaning: start offering puppy food soaked in water at 6 weeks; fully weaned by 8 weeks

Socialization: start as early as possible to prevent puppies from being nervous as an adult

Index

A

AAFCO 53, 54, 101, 117
accessories 22
accident 64
Adenovirus 96
adopt 23, 31, 119
age 6, 101
AKC 3, 4, 10, 11, 16, 23, 33, 78, 79, 82, 83, 84, 98, 113, 118, 119
American Kennel Club 3
American Maltese Association 33, 34
antibiotics 87, 92
antibodies 76
anxious 9
appearance 3, 4, 5
attention 9, 10, 20, 30
award 3

B

bad breath 91
bathing 69
bed 100
behavior 4
behaviors 71
bitch 4, 5
blind 43, 88, 93
blood sugar 89
body 5, 6
Bordatella 96
bowls 22, 25, 84, 100

breed3, 1, 2, 4, 5, 6, 8, 9, 10, 11, 13, 14, 15, 17, 20, 21, 24, 25, 29, 31, 33, 34, 35, 37, 46, 51, 56, 58, 65, 70, 72, 73, 76, 78, 79, 80, 81, 82, 83, 84, 85, 86, 87, 88, 94, 97, 98, 120

breed standard 79, 82
breeder 23, 24, 31, 32, 33, 36, 37, 38, 39, 41, 117
breeding 5, 6, 15, 32, 36, 37, 38, 71, 72, 79, 97
brush 5, 100
brushing 69

C

cage 4, 22
calories 51
Canine Influenza 96
carbohydrate 51, 101
carbohydrates 101
care 3
care sheet 97
castrate 5
chewing 24, 47, 91
children 10, 12, 20, 30, 59, 98
Classic Bob 68
clinic 25
clipping 22
coat 3, 1, 4, 5, 6, 7, 10, 11, 27, 30, 40, 55, 65, 67, 68, 80, 83, 98, 120
Collapsed Trachea 86, 87
collar 24, 25, 28, 100
color 5, 6, 11, 15, 59, 72, 80, 94, 98
coloration 6
coloring 4
colors 6
colostrum 76
comb 5, 47, 66, 100
command 5
companion 2, 9, 14, 21, 29, 65, 79
condition 5

costs	17, 22, 24, 25, 26, 28, 117, 119
coughing	87
crate	23, 25, 84, 100
crate training	58
cut	68, 69

D

dam	4, 6
depressed	9
diabetes	89
diarrhea	39
diet	26, 51, 56, 75, 85, 95, 102, 118, 119
discharge	40, 72
disease	12, 19, 23, 91, 93, 94, 99, 117
disorder	5
Distemper	96
dog bed	100
dog food	50, 53, 56
dog license	18
dogs	3, 1, 3, 4, 5, 8, 9, 10, 12, 15, 17, 18, 20, 21, 23, 26, 29, 30, 32, 33, 37, 44, 46, 51, 54, 56, 57, 59, 60, 68, 70, 71, 72, 73, 74, 75, 78, 79, 83, 86, 87, 88, 89, 90, 91, 92, 93, 94, 99, 117, 118, 119, 120
double coat	4

E

ear	4, 6
ears	5, 10, 11, 12, 40, 69, 77, 79, 80, 98, 102
eating	7
environment	45, 70, 83
estrus cycle	72, 73
exercise	10, 12, 46, 84, 87, 99, 100
eye	3
eyes	3, 10, 11, 40, 77, 79, 93, 98, 102

F

face 3
facts 2, 8, 120
fat 51, 52, 55
fats 101
feeding 50, 56, 85, 118
female 3, 4, 5, 6, 71, 72, 73, 74, 90
fertile 72
food 7, 15, 22, 23, 25, 26, 27, 28, 41, 43, 45, 46, 48, 50, 53, 54, 55, 56, 77, 89, 91, 100, 103
foot 6

G

games 100
gene 3
genealogy 6
genetic 5
gestation period 74
glaucoma 11, 12, 88, 99
glucose 89
groomer 67, 69
grooming 22, 25, 26, 27, 28, 30, 46, 47, 65, 66, 69, 84, 100
growth 6
gum disease 91

H

hair 3, 4, 5, 6, 10, 40, 67, 68, 70, 76, 79, 80
harness 100
health 4, 117, 118
health problems 11, 85, 86
healthy 117
heat 67, 72, 73

herding	100
hip	5
Hip Dysplasia	5
history	8, 13, 14, 15, 37, 92, 94, 117
hobby breeder	36
house	3, 4
housebreaking	58
hyperglycemia	11, 12, 99
Hypothyroidism	12, 99

I

illness	40
information	3, 8, 17, 24, 33, 37, 71, 84, 97, 118
ingredients	54, 55, 101
initial costs	22
intelligent	12, 99

K

kennel	4
Kennel Club	13, 15, 33, 82

L

labor	75, 76
leash	25, 100
legs	5
Leptospirosis	96
lethargic	39
license	18, 26, 27, 28, 37
licensing requirements	17, 18
lifespan	9, 11
litter	7, 31, 32, 39, 74, 76

M

macronutrients	51
male	5, 6, 72, 73, 74, 90
markings	6
microchipping	22
milk	7
minerals	51, 52, 101
money	25
monthly costs	22

N

nails	69
needs	10, 12, 22, 23, 45, 46, 50, 51, 52, 54, 95, 97, 99, 118
neuter	22, 25
nursing	76
nutrients	118

O

obedience training	58
origins	13
outer coat	7

P

Parainfluenza	96
parent	4, 6
Parvovirus	96
patellar luxation	11, 12, 90, 99
Periodontal Disease	86, 91
personality	3, 1, 2, 9, 10, 33, 39, 120
pet	2, 9, 14, 26, 29, 32, 33, 40, 50, 53, 68, 79, 100, 117, 118, 119

Pet Poison Control	57
pets	117
physical	2, 120
portosystemic shunt	11, 12, 92, 99
positive reinforcement	58, 61
pregnant	72, 74
preservatives	55, 101
problems	11, 32, 41, 70, 85, 88, 93
progressive retinal atrophy	11, 12, 93, 99
pros and cons	17, 29
protective	9, 10, 12, 20, 98
protein	51, 52, 54, 101
puppies	5, 7, 20, 32, 37, 38, 39, 40, 59, 63, 73, 74, 75, 76, 77, 102, 103
puppy	23, 28, 101, 103, 117, 119
puppy clip	68
puppy mill	32
puppy playpen	48
puppy proofing	42
puppy-proofing	119
purebred	3

Q

qualities	2, 120

R

rabies	18, 95
record	6
registry	3
reward	61, 62, 64

S

safety	31, 46

separation anxiety 9
sex 25
shaker dog syndrome 11, 94
shampoo 66, 67
shelter 22, 23, 24, 31, 32, 33
show 2, 3, 15, 23, 27, 29, 65, 68, 69, 78, 79, 82, 83, 84, 91
sire 4, 6
size 1, 11, 14, 15, 23, 47, 56, 63, 74, 76, 79, 86
skin 4, 6, 24
skull 3
slicker brush 47
socialization 9, 10, 20, 21, 59
spay 5, 22, 25
Spitz 14
standard 15, 68, 78, 79, 83
strangers 10, 12, 29, 98
supplies 22, 25, 66, 84, 100
surgery 6, 22, 25, 33, 90, 92
swollen 41

T

tail 4, 5, 10, 80
Teddy Bear cut 68
teeth 3, 11, 47, 69, 70, 79, 91, 102
temperature 75, 94, 102
tips 117
toxic 57
toys 22, 28, 100
tracheal collapse 87
train 100
training 9, 20, 21, 22, 23, 29, 33, 47, 58, 61, 62, 63
treatment 20, 86, 87, 88, 89, 91, 94
treats 27, 84
tricks 9
trim 5

trimming 4

U

undercoat 4
undercoat rake 100
urine marking 71

V

vaccination 96
vaccination schedule 85, 95, 96
vaccinations 22, 24, 38, 83, 85, 95, 96
vaccine 18, 96
veterinarian 27
veterinary 26
veterinary care 22, 85, 95
vision 88, 89, 93
vitamins 51, 52, 101, 119

W

walk 10, 12, 24, 41, 46, 53, 90, 99, 100
watch dog 10
water 22, 23, 25, 84, 100, 101, 103
weigh 9, 76
weight 100, 101
whelping 75, 76
white 3, 1, 3, 4, 6, 10, 11, 15, 40, 79, 80, 94, 98, 116, 120
wire pin brush 100
wire-pin brush 47

Maltese Dogs as Pets

Photo Credits

Cover Page Photo By SheltieBoy via Wikimedia Commons, <https://en.wikipedia.org/wiki/File:01_AKC_Maltese_Dog_Show_2013.jpg>

Page 1 Photo By Ann via Wikimedia Commons,<https://en.wikipedia.org/wiki/File:Emily_Maltese.jpg>

Page 8 Photo By ManuelFD via Wikimedia Commons, <https://en.wikipedia.org/wiki/File:Cachorro_de_Bichon_Maltes.JPG>

Page 13 Photo By Flickr User Sscornelius, <https://www.flickr.com/photos/sscornelius/3589962954/sizes/l>

Page 17 Photo By Ed Yourdon via Wikimedia Commons, <https://en.wikipedia.org/wiki/File:A_cute_Maltese_dog.jpg

Page 31 Photo By Pwnsey via Wikimedia Commons, <https://en.wikipedia.org/wiki/File:Maltese_with_Short_Hair_in_Bike_Basket.jpg>

Page 36 Photo By Flickr User Kitty.Green66, <https://www.flickr.com/photos/53887959@N07/4985420598/sizes/l>

Page 42 Photo By Flickr user HazelthePikachu, <https://www.flickr.com/photos/80435089@N08/7722827902/sizes/l>

Page 45 Photo By Ann via Wikimedia Commons, <https://commons.wikimedia.org/wiki/File:Double_your_fun_(Maltese)..jpg>

Page 48 Photo By Flickr user Lianaagh, <https://www.flickr.com/photos/write-pudding/2783595828/sizes/o/>

Page 50 Photo By Arvin5200 via Wikimedia Commons, <https://commons.wikimedia.org/wiki/File:Maltese_dog_named_Pofak.jpg>

Page 53 Photo By Flickr user Tiarescott, <https://www.flickr.com/photos/tiarescott/33336635/sizes/o/>

Page 58 Photo By Yazmapaz via Wikimedia Commons, <https://commons.wikimedia.org/wiki/File:Maltese_puppy_blue_bow.jpg>

Page 61 Photo By Flickr user Abby Lanes, <https://www.flickr.com/photos/abbylanes/3432190593/sizes/l>

Page 65 Photo By Flickr user Ann Gordon, <https://www.flickr.com/photos/75976921@N00/1038598547/sizes/o/>

Page 71 Photo By Yasmapaz via Wikimedia Commons, <https://commons.wikimedia.org/wiki/File:Maltese_puppy_portrait.jpg>

Page 74 Photo By Yazmapaz & Ace_Heart via Wikimedia Commons, <https://commons.wikimedia.org/wiki/File:Maltese_puppy,_3_days_old.jpg>

Page 78 Photo By Flickr user Andymako, <https://www.flickr.com/photos/andymako/15866956238/sizes/l>

Page 82 Photo By Flickr user Golbenge, <https://www.flickr.com/photos/golbenge/4909684031/sizes/l>

Page 85 Photo By Pixabay User Pezibear, <https://pixabay.com/en/dog-maltese-young-animal-young-dog-1122997/>

Page 95 Photo By Pixabay User Pezibear, <https://pixabay.com/en/dog-white-maltese-puppy-1037702/>

Page 97 Photo By Flickr User Wsilver, <https://www.flickr.com/photos/psycho-pics/3411848285/sizes/l>

References

"AAFCO Dog Food Nutrient Profiles." DogFoodAdvisor. <http://www.dogfoodadvisor.com/frequently-asked-questions/aafco-nutrient-profiles/>

"Annual Dog Care Costs." PetFinder. <https://www.petfinder.com/pet-adoption/dog-adoption/annual-dog-care-costs/>

"Canine Dental Disease." Banfield Pet Hospital. <http://www.banfield.com/pet-health-resources/preventive-care/dental/canine-dental-disease>

"Choosing a Healthy Puppy." WebMD. <http://pets.webmd.com/dogs/guide/choosing-healthy-puppy>

"Grooming Maltese Dogs." Maltese Only. <http://www.malteseonly.com/page2.html>

"How to Find a Responsible Breeder." HumaneSociety.org. <http://www.humanesociety.org/issues/puppy_mills/tips/finding_responsible_dog_breeder.html?referrer=https://www.google.com/>

"Maltese." PetMD. <http://www.petmd.com/dog/breeds/c_dg_maltese>

"Maltese." VetStreet.com. <http://www.vetstreet.com/dogs/maltese#history>

"Maltese Dog Breed Information." DogTime.com. <http://dogtime.com/dog-breeds/maltese>

"Maltese History." PetMaltese.com. <http://www.petmaltese.com/Maltese_History.html>

"Maltese Puppy Size." Maltese Mystique. <http://www.mymaltese.com/Pages/PuppySize.aspx>

"Maltese Temperament." Your Purebred Puppy. <http://www.yourpurebredpuppy.com/reviews/maltese.html>

"Most Popular Dog Breeds in America." AKC.org. <http://www.akc.org/news/the-most-popular-dog-breeds-in-america/>

"My Bowl: What Goes into a Balanced Diet for Your Dog?" PetMD. <http://www.petmd.com/dog/slideshows/nutrition-center/my-bowl-what-goes-into-a-balanced-diet-for-your-dog>

"Nutrients Your Dog Needs." ASPCA.org. <https://www.aspca.org/pet-care/dog-care/nutrients-your-dog-needs>

"Nutrition: General Feeding Guidelines for Dogs." VCA Animal Hospitals. <http://www.vcahospitals.com/main/pet-health-information/article/animal-health/nutrition-general-feeding-guidelines-for-dogs/6491>

"Official Standard of the Maltese." AKC.org. <http://cdn.akc.org/Maltese.pdf?_ga=1.183104230.1751144016.1454425532>

"Pet Care Costs." ASPCA.org. <https://www.aspca.org/adopt/pet-care-costs>

"Puppy Proofing Your Home." Hill's Pet. <http://www.hillspet.com/dog-care/puppy-proofing-your-home.html>

"Puppy Proofing Your Home." PetEducation.com. <http://www.peteducation.com/article.cfm?c=2+2106&aid=3283>

"Types of Maltese Haircuts." The Nest Pets. <http://pets.thenest.com/types-maltese-haircuts-6065.html>

Vitamins and Minerals Your Dog Needs." Kim Boatman. The Dog Daily. <http://www.thedogdaily.com/dish/diet/dogs_vitamins/index.html#.VHOtMPnF_IA>

"Why a Maltese Should Be Your Dog of Choice." TerrificPets.com. <http://www.terrificpets.com/articles/10227165.asp>

More Titles Available...

Feeding Baby
Cynthia Cherry
978-1941070000

Axolotl
Lolly Brown
978-0989658430

Dysautonomia, POTS Syndrome
Frederick Earlstein
978-0989658485

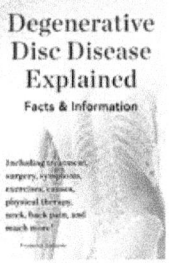

Degenerative Disc Disease Explained
Frederick Earlstein
978-0989658485

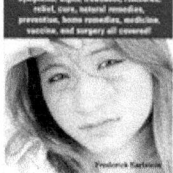

Sinusitis, Hay Fever,
Allergic Rhinitis Explained
Frederick Earlstein
978-1941070024

Wicca
Riley Star
978-1941070130

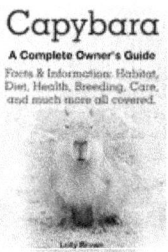

Zombie Apocalypse
Rex Cutty
978-1941070154

Capybara
Lolly Brown
978-1941070062

Eels As Pets
Lolly Brown
978-1941070167

Scabies and Lice Explained
Frederick Earlstein
978-1941070017

Saltwater Fish As Pets
Lolly Brown
978-0989658461

Torticollis Explained
Frederick Earlstein
978-1941070055

Kennel Cough
Lolly Brown
978-0989658409

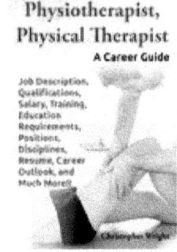

Physiotherapist, Physical Therapist
Christopher Wright
978-0989658492

Rats, Mice, and Dormice As Pets
Lolly Brown
978-1941070079

Wallaby and Wallaroo Care
Lolly Brown
978-1941070031

Bodybuilding Supplements
Explained
Jon Shelton
978-1941070239

Demonology
Riley Star
978-19401070314

Pigeon Racing
Lolly Brown
978-1941070307

Dwarf Hamster
Lolly Brown
978-1941070390

Cryptozoology
Rex Cutty
978-1941070406

Eye Strain
Frederick Earlstein
978-1941070369

Inez The Miniature Elephant
Asher Ray
978-1941070353

Vampire Apocalypse
Rex Cutty
978-1941070321

www.ingramcontent.com/pod-product-compliance
Lightning Source LLC
Chambersburg PA
CBHW071705040426
42446CB00011B/1918